The Rye & Camber Tramway

Peter A. Harding

A general view of Rye Station, looking towards Camber. 11th April 1931.   H.C. Casserley

Published by Peter A. Harding,
Mossgiel, Bagshot Road, Knaphill,
Woking, Surrey GU21 2SG.

ISBN 0 9509414 1 7

© Peter A. Harding 1985

Printed by Binfield Printers Ltd.,
Binfield Road, Byfleet, Surrey.

Contents

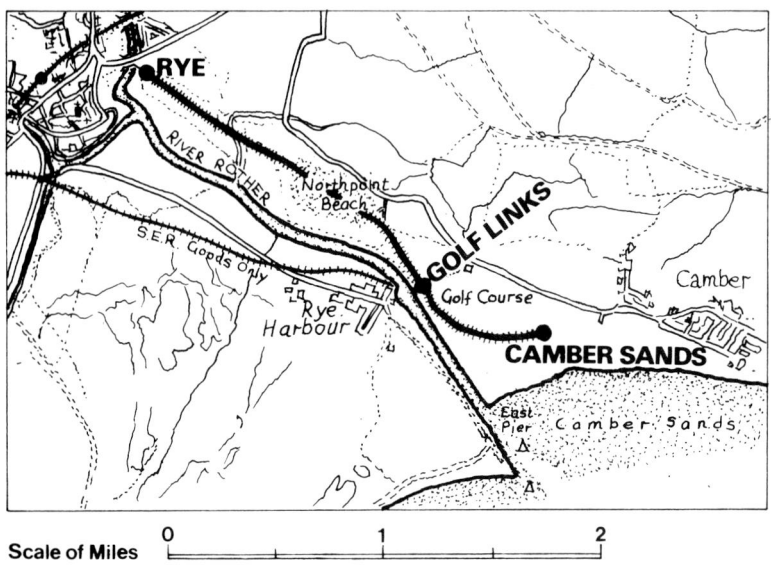

Scale of Miles 0   1   2

The petrol locomotive pulling both carriages and the open passenger wagons towards Golf Links Station on the slight embankment from Camber Sands. 12th July 1931. H.C. Casserley

Introduction

Anyone unfamiliar with the Rye & Camber Tramway might be surprised to find that it was not a typical street tramway but was, in fact, a rather unique 3 ft gauge steam railway which followed its own right of way and was later to become one of this country's first conversions from steam to petrol.

The line was built on private land and therefore did not require any Parliamentary powers and was opened in 1895 from a terminus near the Monkbretton Bridge at Rye to the then recently opened Rye Golf Club near Camber.

Primarily for use by the golfers the tramway was also of great use to the fishing community at Rye Harbour who were able to get to work via a ferry across the River Rother from the original Camber terminus which was later renamed Golf Links Station.

The tram (as it was so affectionately called) was also to become popular with day trippers to the endless sand dunes at Camber and in 1908 the line was extended to a new terminus just short of Camber itself and suitably named Camber Sands.

When World War II broke out in 1939 the line was closed, but as the Admiralty was involved in building a 1000 ft continuous jetty on the Camber side of the River Rother opposite Rye Harbour, the tramway was requisitioned and put to use for carrying men and materials between Rye and the Golf Links Station.

After the war the line was handed back to its owners but, as the track and rolling stock were in such a dilapidated state it was decided to wind up the company.

Today, the tram, which was such a familiar sight to so many people is now just a fading memory, but to those who do remember, I hope that this booklet will be a gentle reminder of those far off days and those happy rides to Camber.

2-4-0 T "Victoria" with both the carriages at Rye. Conductor/guard Percy Sheppard appears to be organising the passengers on the platform. 18th July 1914.

L.C.G.B. Ken Nunn Collection

History of the Line

The picturesque old Cinque Port town of Rye stands on a hill overlooking the flat marsh and the River Rother which is joined just below the town by the River Tillingham.

Some two miles south of Rye at the mouth of the River Rother is the village of Rye Harbour which is situated on the west bank. In March 1854 the South Eastern Railway opened a standard gauge, single track branch to Rye Harbour from their main Ashford to Hastings line at a point just south of Rye Station. Although this line served the harbour, it was always worked as a freight only siding and never carried passengers.

In 1894 the Rye Golf Club was opened amidst the sand dunes towards Camber on the other side of the Rother from the harbour and at about this time a group of Rye businessmen decided to form a company with a view to constructing a short railway line from Rye to a terminus on the east bank of the Rother at the side of the new golf course opposite Rye Harbour so that it could serve not only the golfers but also the harbour community by way of a ferry.

After several meetings at which Mr. Cuthbert Hayles was appointed Chairman and Mr. H.G. Henbrey appointed Secretary, the Rye and Camber Tramways Company Limited was registered on the 6th April 1895 with a capital of £2,300 which was to be used not only for building the line and both stations but also to obtain an engine and carriage to work it. The Rye Town Council agreed to lease a small piece of land at the south-east corner of the Monkbretton Bridge (on the other side of the Rother from Rye) at £2 a year for 21 years so that a station building and engine shed could be built.

The company appointed Mr. Holman F. Stephens as engineer and he not only designed the line but was also responsible for equipping it. Stephens (who was later to become the celebrated Lt. Colonel Stephens) was still in his twenties at the time and had in fact hoped to work the line with what he described in a letter to the Railway Department of the Board of Trade as an "oil motor on a passenger car bogie". If he had been successful it would have probably been the first "diesel" type vehicle on any passenger carrying railway in the world which would have certainly made this little line famous, but unfortunately the cost and experimental time were too much for such a small undertaking whose main aim was to open the line as soon as possible. As it was, the company had already ordered from Messrs. W.G. Bagnall Ltd., of Stafford, a small steam locomotive which was a 2-4-0 tank and was appropriately called "Camber" plus a carriage which was divided into first and second class sections by a partition. Also acquired at the time of opening were two rather flimsy-looking wagons. The contractors appointed to lay the track and erect the two station buildings were Messrs. Mancktelow Bros. of Horsmonden.

The track which was single throughout with run round loops at both the stations was 3ft gauge and was made of 26lb Vignoles rails spiked to creosoted wooden sleepers.

The fact that it was called a tramway and not a railway was probably because it was built on private land and did not require any Parliamentary powers. It also managed to be built a year before the passing of the Light Railway Act of 1896. If it had been built after the 1896 Act it could well have been called a light railway even though it was built on private land, as to all intents and purposes it was a light railway and ran on the one engine in steam principle which meant that the line did not require any signals.

The grand opening ceremony of the tramway took place on Saturday 13th July,

1895 when the Mayor & Mayoress of Rye and a specially invited party of guests gathered on the platform of the new Rye Tram Station (as it was to be called) where the Mayoress of Rye, Mrs. F. Bellingham declared the line open and received a bouquet from Miss Marion Vidler.

To the sound of fog signals and cheers from a number of townspeople who had gathered around the station to watch, the first party of invited guests rattled merrily on their way to the Camber terminus while the rest waited for the train to return before they, too, could sample the delights of the new line.

When the whole party had completed the 1½ mile journey to the Camber terminus they all strolled across the golf course to the Royal William Hotel where, in the true English tradition for any such event, luncheon was served.

Those present at the luncheon which was presided over by the Chairman of the Company, Mr. Cuthbert Hayles were Alderman & Mrs. F. Bellingham (Mayor & Mayoress of Rye), Mr. G.M. Freeman (Mayor of Winchelsea) and Miss Freeman, Mrs. C. Hayles, Mr. H.G. Henbrey (Company Secretary), Colonel & Mrs. Brookfield, Rev. A.J.W. Crosse (Vicar of Rye), Mr. R.P. Burra and Miss Burra, Mr. J. Symonds Vidler, Dr. E.W. Skinner, Dr. & Mrs. A.E. Vidler, Mr. & Mrs. T.G. Sharpe, Dr. J.R. Skinner and Miss Skinner, Mr. Kelly, Mr. Humphreys, Mr. W. Carless, Mr. J. Howell, Mr. T. Busby, Mr. C.A. Selmes, Mr. & Mrs. F.H. Chapman, Mr. & Mrs. A.E. Hinds, Mr. & Mrs. W. Fuller, Mr. W.G. Rubie (Sen.) and Miss Rubie, Mr. H. Smith, Mr. W. Wright, Mr. C. Fletcher, (Sen.), Mr. J.L. Deacon, Mrs. W.T. Smith, Miss Payne, Mr. J. Adams, Mr. J.M. Jenkins, Mr. H. Bond, Mr. & Mrs. W. Dawes, Mr. W. Martindale, Mr. & Mrs. J.N. Masters, Mr. A. Smith, Mr. & Mrs. H.J. Gasson, Mr. W. Neeves and Mr. Mancktelow (Contractor).

Mr. Cuthbert Hayles, on behalf of the company, thanked everyone present for the compliments they had paid him personally and the tramway in general and went on to propose a toast to Mr. H.F. Stephens (the engineer) and the contractors (Messrs. Mancktelow Bros.) and also to Mr. E.P.S. Jones of the Rother Iron Works who was responsible for transporting the engine and carriage promptly from the main line even though they had only arrived at noon the previous day.

It was regretted that out of a sense of duty Messrs. Stephens and Jones were still at work on the line and were unable to attend the luncheon.

After the luncheon the party separated to enjoy a game of golf, or a stroll over the links or on the Camber sands before the return journey to Rye.

The entire stock of the line at the time of opening in 1895.   R.L. Innes Collection

5

The fare for a first class ticket when the line was opened was 4d single and 6d return. Second class was 2d single and 4d return and season tickets were also obtainable, being mainly used by the golfers. The fishermen had an annual season ticket at the rate of 30s for the whole crew of a boat.

A parcels service was also provided by the company who, in addition, provided a small parcel delivery service to Rye Harbour Village at a standard charge of 4d (which included tramway, ferry and delivery).

On the first August Bank Holiday after the opening, the day's takings amounted to £12-5s and during the first six months 18,000 tickets were sold and a dividend of 7½ per cent was declared.

This early success prompted the directors to obtain another engine and also another carriage. The new carriage arrived in 1896 and was built locally by Mr. E.P.S. Jones of the Rother Ironworks at Rye and was also a bogie coach and accommodated 25 third class passengers. The new engine was delivered in 1897 and was another 2-4-0 tank similar to "Camber" although slightly larger and was also obtained from Messrs. W.G. Bagnall Ltd. of Stafford. It was named "Victoria".

The rather flimsy-looking goods wagons were replaced in 1900 by some sturdier, more conventional types.

In 1901 a standard gauge light railway was authorised from the Rother Valley Railway at Northiam to the South Eastern & Chatham Railway Station at Rye and was to be called the East Sussex Light Railway. Section 38 of this Light Railway Order gave the East Sussex Light Railway powers to repair, maintain and work the Rye & Camber Tramway, subject to agreement, even though there was to be no physical rail connection.

A trial run just before the official opening of the line at Rye with W.H. Austen (Assistant to Holman F. Stephens) in white trousers acting as driver.   D.A. Boreham Collection

6

This scheme came to nothing and the East Sussex Light Railway was never built, so the Rye & Camber Tramway was left to continue on its own at a time when, despite its popularity, the finances of the company were quite precarious. They were now depending on subsidies from the Rye Golf Club to help balance the books and in 1901 the Golf Club contributed £25 to compensate for the loss on Sunday running which the company was experiencing at the time. In 1902 a subsidy of £10 was paid in order to keep the tramway operational during the five winter months.

In its issue dated 10th October 1903 the Sussex Express reported: "Some weeks ago we announced the decision of the directors of the Rye & Camber Tramway not to run their steam cars throughout the winter months unless they receive a subsidy of £50. Since then the matter has been put before the various clubs in the town, with the result that, at a meeting of the directors on Saturday, the Secretary was able to state that the Golf, Mermaid and Dormy Clubs had guaranteed to pay two-thirds of the amount required, whilst the Mayor (Dr. Skinner) had guaranteed the other third. Accordingly the trams will run as hitherto and the Mayor's generous action will earn the gratitude of the townspeople. The Mayor's action is not, however, without precedent for in 1900 the then Mayor (Ald. F. Jarrett), benefited the town in a similar manner." This subsidy also enabled caddies and workmen to travel for 1d.

By 1906 things were better and the books showed a credit balance of £246 5s 10d which resulted in the directors announcing a 4 per cent dividend.

After much discussion, the company decided to extend the line to a new terminus nearer the sands to cater for the ever-increasing day trippers who were now arriving for a day on the sands.

2-4-0T "Camber" at the original Camber terminus (later renamed Golf Links Station) before the extension to Camber Sands was built. The ER of the Camber Station name board can just be seen through the front of the carriage. (Above the head of the gentleman standing by the track).   Lens of Sutton

The cost of the extension was £650 and the new terminus which was called Camber Sands was advertised as being "far from the madding crowd". The original Camber terminus was then renamed and was given the more realistic title of Golf Links. The grand opening of the extension was on Monday 13th July 1908 (exactly 13 years to the day when the original line was opened). The opening ceremony was in fact carried out by the "Tram" itself by breaking a silken cord stretched across the line at the old terminus.

A large crowd gathered on the new Camber Sands Station which was just a raised wooden platform and among those present were Mr. Cuthbert Hayles (Chairman), Mr. R.H. Hunnisett (Managing Director), Alderman J.N. Masters, Rev. W.M. Manning, Mr. F. Jarrett, Mr. A.A. Clark J.P., Mr. G. Ellis J.P., Mr. W. Dawes and Mr. E.P. Dawes. Later the party returned to the aptly named "Retreat" where tea was served.

The new extension was put to great use during the summer months, but as the business was mainly seasonal the restricted winter service would terminate at the Golf Links Station although sometimes a couple of the trucks would be taken down to Camber Sands, filled with sand and then taken back to Rye where the sand was sold to local builders.

The drop in income during the winter months still added to the cash flow problems and the company still needed subsidies from the Golf Club who gave £48 in 1914 and then settled at £25 from 1917 to 1924. The £38 subsidy in 1925 was the last paid by the Golf Club and after that the company had to struggle along on its own.

In the same year, by way of an experiment, the company introduced a petrol locomotive which was obtained from the Kent Construction Company of Ashford and even though it was often compared with an overgrown lawnmower it proved to be quite successful. In fact it was so successful that "Victoria" was soon sold for scrap and "Camber" was to languish in the shed at Rye and was rarely used.

Mr. Charles A. Gafford had become Secretary to the company in the early 1900's and was soon to become the Managing Director with full responsibility for the administration of the line and was to remain in this capacity until the line closed in 1939.

The Chairman of the company in later years was Mr. C. Ashton Selmes.

The scene at Camber Sands Station on the 13th July 1908 at the opening of the extension.

The Lines Engineer

Holman F. Stephens (1868-1931)

Having completed his first appointment as resident engineer to the Cranbrook &
Paddock Wood Railway in 1893, Holman F. Stephens was appointed at the age of
27 by the Directors of the Rye & Camber Tramway to engineer their interesting little
line and this he did in a very short time.

As previously mentioned, Stephens not only designed the line but he also had plans
to work it with an "oil motor on a passenger bogie car." What he actually planned is
still vague, but it seems that he was seriously considering using an internal
combustion locomotive based on the Akroyd Stuart principle, although a Priestman
engine has also been suggested.

Unlike the line, Stephens' plan to work it with an internal combustion engine never
saw the light of day and the tramway opened with the conventional steam
locomotive "Camber" and the bogie carriage.

Holman F. Stephens was born in Hammersmith, London on the 31st October 1868
and was the son of F.G. Stephens (who was art critic of the Athenaeum). He studied
civil engineering in London under Sir Alexander Kennedy. He also studied in
Germany. Later he joined the Metropolitan Railway at Neasden where he worked
under J.J. Hanbury.

When in his early twenties he set out on his long career as an engineer with his first
appointment to the Cranbrook & Paddock Wood Railway and after short com-
missions with the Cranbrook & District Water Company and also the Medway
Navigation, he followed up with his appointment to the Rye & Camber Tramway.

After the passing of the Light Railway Act of 1896, Stephens was to become
involved with various light railways all over the country and in fact engineered the
first light railway to be constructed under the provisions of the 1896 Act which was
the Rother Valley Railway running from Robertsbridge to Tenterden. When the line
was extended from Tenterden to Headcorn it was renamed the Kent & East Sussex
Railway and as well as being the lines engineer, Stephens also became the
Managing Director.

He went on to manage several of the lines he engineered and with other lines that
he either reconstructed or acquired, he formed a group which he controlled from an
office at Salford Terrace, Tonbridge.

The other companies which formed the group were the East Kent Light Railway,
the Hundred of Manhood & Selsey Tramway (later called the West Sussex
Railway), the Shropshire & Montgomeryshire Light Railway, the Weston, Clevedon
& Portishead Railway, the Festiniog Railway, the Welsh Highland Railway and the
Snailbeach & District Railway. He also built and managed the Plymouth, Devonport

& South Western Junction Railway but was later to resign from this position.

The Rye & Camber Tramway was never to form any part of the group but, without being involved with the general running of the line, Stephens continued to advise the tramway. It's also interesting to note that he was to have been the engineer to the proposed East Sussex Light Railway which would have run from Northiam to Rye and, subject to agreement, could have had the powers to repair, maintain and work the Rye & Camber Tramway.

Other lines that he engineered but did not form any part of his group were the Sheppey Light Railway, the Burry Port & Gwendraeth Valley Railway, the Ashover Light Railway, the Edge Hill Light Railway, the North Devon & Cornwall Junction Railway and also, of course, the Cranbrook & Paddock Wood Railway.

While starting out with the Cranbrook & Paddock Wood Railway, Stephens seems to have developed the corrugated style station buildings which became synonymous with his work in years to come (even though they varied slightly from line to line) and although the contractor J.T. Firbank of East Grinstead was responsible for the permanent way from Paddock Wood to Hawkhurst, Stephens became associated with Mancktelow Bros. of Horsmonden with regard to the actual station buildings.

When it came to building the Rye & Camber Tramway on a very tight budget, Mancktelow Bros. were given the task of laying the track and building the two station buildings.

Stephens continued his association with Mancktelow Bros. when in 1897 they were appointed engineer and contractor respectively to the Hundred of Manhood & Selsey Tramway.

When Stephens died in October 1931 his group of light railways was taken over by Mr. W.H. Austen who had been a friend and assistant since they both started on the Cranbrook & Paddock Wood Railway when Austen was in his early teens. After Stephens' death, W.H. Austen continued to advise the Rye & Camber Tramway until it closed in 1939.

2-4-0T "Camber" and both carriages at Rye. c. 1905. The permanent way trolley can also be seen.   Miss B. Rhodes Collection

Description of the Route

Although slightly smaller, the station building at Rye was very typical of the stations that Holman F. Stephens had built for the Cranbrook & Paddock Wood Railway (particularly Horsmonden and Hawkhurst), even down to the ornate barge boards. It was made of corrugated iron on wooden frames with an awning on two wooden supports using V-shaped joints.

The building which later had the words "Tram Station" painted in large white letters on the roof (so that it could be easily seen from the town of Rye) consisted of a waiting room and a booking office, although the latter was only used in the early days because tickets were mostly sold by a conductor/guard.

An engine and carriage shed which was also made of corrugated iron was built across the end of the line and later a similar double shed was added slightly to the rear of the station building.

As with other stations on the line there was only one platform and at Rye it was a solid type of brick and concrete. When the station was opened there was a wooden lattice fence at the back of the platform each side of the station building but, as the station was modified, the fencing was replaced.

There was a loop for the engine to run round the carriages and the points were worked by a balance-weight lever.

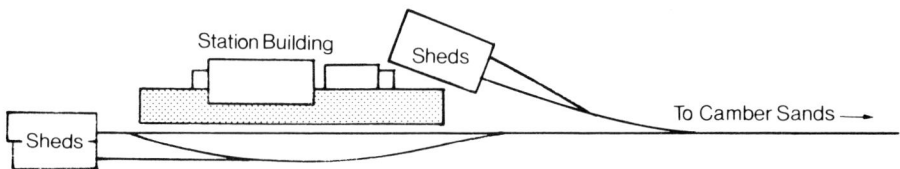

RYE STATION

Rye Station.   Lens of Sutton

On leaving Rye the line ran dead straight across the flat fields and was fenced in for some way with an iron fence similar to the type found on country estates. After about ½ mile the line crossed the Broadwater stream by a bridge and then continued across a shingle area known as the Northpoint Beach before passing first a house called Gorse Cottage and then another house which has often been referred to as the Halfway House but in fact was originally built by a squatter and was named Golf View, then Beachlands and finally Squatter's Right. Although there was no platform here the train (or tram as it was always called) would stop at this point by request.

2-4-0T "Victoria" and both carriages crossing the Broadwater Bridge heading towards Rye. 18th July 1914. L.C.G.B. Ken Nunn Collection

The tram on its way to Rye passing Golf View at about the turn of the century. Golf View was later renamed Beachlands and finally Squatter's Right. Lens of Sutton

From here the line ran past the small cottage on the left which was occupied by Charles Tunbridge (who was Harbour-master at Rye Harbour from 1915 to 1925) and then gave the passengers a fine view of the mouth of the River Rother and Rye Harbour on the right before arriving at Golf Links Station.

Golf Links Station was a very similar building to Rye Station but without any engine and carriage sheds. It was a typical Stephens-style corrugated iron construction and like Rye there was also a solid platform and a wooden lattice fence at the back of the platform, but, unlike Rye, the fence was to last throughout most of the station's existence.

This was, of course, the original terminus and had a run round loop, but when the extension was opened to Camber Sands in 1908 the loop was rarely used and by the early 1930's it had been removed. (Only to be reinstated by the Admiralty during the Second World War. A siding to the jetty which was built directly opposite the harbour was also added).

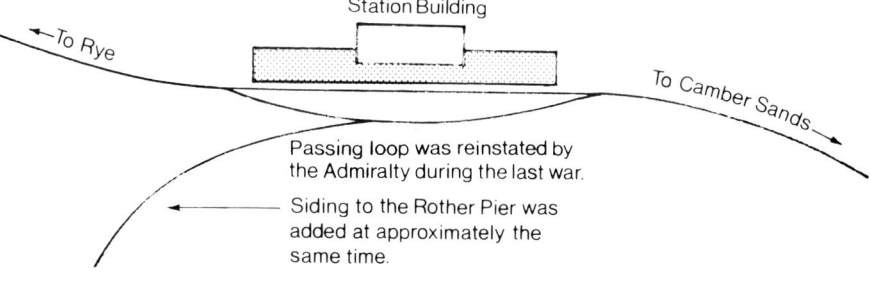

GOLF LINKS STATION

Golf Links Station.

Lens of Sutton

From Golf Links the line took first a sharp right turn and then left and ran along a slight embankment beside part of the golf course before it reached Camber Sands Station. Sometimes when there were floods this part of the line would have water on both sides and passengers must have felt a great sense of excitement as they travelled along this stretch.

Unlike the other two stations on the line, Camber Sands was much simpler and was built of old standard gauge sleepers. At first there was no shelter, but later a small wooden hut was added. A run round loop was also provided for the engine.

As previously mentioned, some of the early time-tables referred to the new terminus as being "far from the madding crowd" and there's no doubt that this statement most certainly applied because the station was over ½ mile from Camber itself and was in an area that never was (or has been) developed.

At one time Thompson's the bakers of Rye had a tea hut next to the station where a bucket and spade could also be purchased, but apart from this and one or two other small huts this sleepy little corner of Sussex could have been mistaken for just about anywhere from the Sahara Desert to the wild west of America.

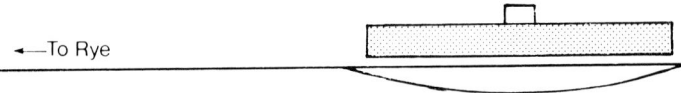

—To Rye

CAMBER SANDS STATION

Camber Sands Station.

Lens of Sutton

Motive Power and Rolling Stock

As already mentioned, to work the line at its commencement the company purchased a small 2-4-0 tank engine and a bogie passenger carriage from W.G. Bagnall Ltd., of Stafford.

The locomotive which bore the Bagnall's number 1461 was named "Camber" and had the following dimensions:

```
Cylinders........................... 5½ in x 9 in
Leading wheels..................... 1 ft diameter
Driving wheels..................... 1 ft 8 in diameter
Tank capacity...................... 120 gallons
Heating surface:
    Tubes.......................... 55 sq ft
    Firebox ....................... 12 sq ft
Grate area......................... 2.5 sq ft
Weight in working order............ 6 tons
```

The piston rods and crossheads were encased to protect them from the sand that blows across the Camber district. Its normal speed was 10 m.p.h. but it could reach 20 m.p.h. if needed and was said to have been capable of pulling 60 tons on the level. It arrived with a light green livery with black bands and red lining.

The passenger carriage weighed 3 tons and had spoked wheels on two small bogies. It was 25 ft 6 in long, 6 ft 3 in wide and 8 ft 11 in high; the bogies had a wheelbase of 3 ft 6 in and bogie centres were 12 ft 6 in apart. It was divided into first and second class sections by a partition. On the wall of the first class side of the partition was a clock and this section also contained 12 cushioned seats around the sides and along the partition.

The second class section of the carriage had sash windows (which could be completely removed in hot weather) and longitudinal strip-wood seating was provided for 20 passengers. The carriage had a patent centre coupling with no buffers and was equipped with a handbrake and had entrance platforms at both ends. Also at the time of opening the company acquired a couple of rather flimsy-looking goods wagons with spindly little wheels.

2-4-0T "Camber" and 2-4-0T "Victoria" at Rye. 10th April 1909. L.C.G.B. Ken Nunn Collection

In 1896 the second passenger carriage was obtained which was also a bogie carriage and was built by Mr. E.P.S. Jones of the Rother Ironworks at Rye. This vehicle accommodated 25 third class passengers and had an entrance platform at one end only. There were three large windows, capped by ventilators on each side.

In 1897 the company took delivery of a second locomotive which was another 2-4-0 tank engine from Bagnall's. This engine was named "Victoria" and was similar to "Camber" but was slightly larger and bore the maker's number 1511. "Victoria's" dimensions were as follows:

Cylinders	6 in x 10in
Leading wheels	1ft 2in diameter
Driving wheels	2ft ½in diameter
Tank capacity	150 gallons
Heating surface:	
Tubes	103 sq ft
Firebox	15 sq ft
Grate area	3 sq ft
Weight in working order	6 tons 12 cwt

"Victoria's" livery was blue with yellow lining and the pistons and crossheads were encased like those of "Camber".

In 1900 the flimsy-looking goods wagons were replaced by some rather sturdier types whose main function was to carry sand from Camber. During the First World War, two of these wagons were used for carrying ammunition and were nicely finished with leather padding, later these two wagons were adapted and fitted with seats to accommodate extra passengers when the two carriages were full and resembled the type of open-topped passenger carriages used on miniature railways.

In later years both the Bagnall carriage and the Rother Ironworks carriage were rebuilt and the small end platforms were incorporated into the main part of the bodies and the Bagnall carriage also became third class only. As all three stations only had single platforms (on the down side) both carriages and open trucks needed entrances on one side only.

In 1925 the company obtained a four-wheeled petrol locomotive from the Kent Construction Company of Ashford which looked more like a giant sized lawnmower than a railway engine but it proved to be quite a success. When it arrived it had a small half-width cab for the driver who had to sit sideways with his feet exposed. Later the cab was rebuilt to the full width and was also provided with small round windows front and back.

After the petrol locomotive arrived "Victoria" was sold for scrap and although "Camber" remained it was rarely used.

One other important item used on the line was the permanent way trolley which was a "row-boat" type and was used for all maintenance work.

Open top wagons at Rye. 10th April 1909. Note the fabric covers over the grease axleboxes to keep sand out.

L.C.G.B. Ken Nunn Collection

16

The two open top passenger wagons with the petrol locomotive and both the carriages at Camber Sands.

T. Middlemass

The petrol locomotive at Rye.

L.C.G.B. Ken Nunn Collection

Timetables

RYE & CAMBER TRAM SERVICE (Subject to Alterations.)

Week-Days   JUNE, 1908.   Sundays.

LEAVE RYE. A.M.		LEAVE GOLF LINKS. A.M.	LEAVE RYE. A.M.		LEAVE GOLF LINKS. A.M
10 0		10 20	10 0		10 15
11 0		11 20			
12 0		**P.M.**	*Special Fares by 10 a.m. from Rye.*		
P.M.	Parcels are conveyed between Rye and Camber and Rye Harbour at very low Charges.	12 30	**P.M.**		**P.M.**
1 30		1 50	2 0	Camber as a Health Resort is very Invigorating. No one should miss the opportunity of a Visit to the Sands.	2 15
2 0		2 15	2 30		2 45
2 30		2 50	3 0		3 30
3 30		3 40	4 0		4 15
4 40		5 0	4 30		4 45
5 50		6 0	5 30		5 40
6 30		7 0	6 0		6 15
			6 30		6 45

Extra Saturday Trams.

a.m.	a.m.
9 30	9 40
p.m.	**p.m.**
8 0	8 15

Picnic, School, and Pleasure Parties carried at Reduced Fares for Parties of not less than 12 Adults.

Cheap Return Tickets can be obtained at Messrs. ADAMS & SON'S, 7, High Street, Rye.

The Extension to Camber Sands will shortly be opened, when a Supplementary Time Table will be issued.

Parcels are conveyed between Rye and Camber and Rye Harbour at very Low Charges.

RYE & CAMBER TRAM SERVICE (Subject to Alterations

Week-Days   [OCTOBER, 1925

	a.m.	a.m.	p.m.	p.m.	p.m.	p.m.	p.m.	p.m.
Rye	10 0	11 0	12 0	2 0	3 0	4 0	5 0	6 0
Golf Links	10 9	11 9	12 9	2 9	3 9	4 9	5 9	6 9
Camber Sands	1014	1114	1214	2 14	3 14	4 14	5 14	6 14
Camber Sands	1015	1115	1215	2 15	3 15	4 15	5 15	6 15
Golf Links	1020	1120	1220	2 20	3 20	4 20	5 20	6 20
Rye	1030	1130	1230	2 30	3 30	4 30	5 30	6 30

Special Trams between for 12 or more Passengers

Sundays.

	a.m.	a.m.	p.m.	p.m.	p.m.	p.m.	p.m.
Rye ..	.. 10 0	11 0	2 0	3 0	4 0	5 0	6 0
Golf Links	.. 10 9	11 9	2 9	3 9	4 9	5 9	6 9
Camber Sands	.. 1014	1114	2 14	3 14	4 14	5 14	6 14
Camber Sands	.. 1015	1115	2 15	3 15	4 15	5 15	6 15
Golf Links	.. 1020	1120	2 20	3 20	4 20	5 20	6 20
Rye ..	.. 1030	1130	2 30	3 30	4 30	5 30	6 30

Picnic, School, and Pleasure Parties (not less than 12 Adults) carried at Reduced Fares.

Cheap Return Tickets can be obtained at Messrs. Adams & Son's, 7, High Street, Rye.

Camber is a Health Resort is very Invigorating.   No one should miss the opportunity of a Visit to the Sands.

A Selection of Tickets

RYE and CAMBER TRAMWAYS COMPANY, LIMITED. THIRD CLASS Single Fare **3**d. <small>Williamson Ticket Printer, Ashton</small> B 0917	**Rye and Camber Tramways Company, Limited.** SECOND CLASS. Single Fare **4**d. 13384
Rye and Camber Tramways Company, Limited Third Single **Sands** **4**d <small>Williamson, Ticket Printer, Ashton.</small> A 457	**Rye and Camber Tramways Company, Limited** Third Return **SANDS** **7**d <small>Williamson, Ticket Printer, Ashton.</small> F 3472
Rye and Camber Tramways Company, Limited Third Single **GOLF LINKS** **3**d <small>Williamson, Ticket Printer, Ashton.</small> A 2842	**Rye and Camber Tramways Company, Limited** Third Single **GOLF LINKS** **4**d <small>Williamson, Ticket Printer, Ashton.</small> A 8508
Rye and Camber Tramways Company, Limited **CADDIE** **1**d <small>Williamson, Ticket Printer, Ashton.</small> A 8926	**Rye and Camber Tramways Company, Limited.** Caddies' Single Ticket. **1**d. 7824
Rye and Camber Tramways Company, Limited. **DOG** **3**d <small>Williamson, Ticket Printer, Ashton.</small> A 0749	**Rye and Camber Tramways Company, Limited.** THIRD CLASS. Single Fare **1**d. 48352

Life on theTramway

Leisurely journeys across the marsh to Camber on the tramway were very much the order of the day, but for the staff, like driver Albert "Jokey" Rhodes, it was very hard work. Before the First World War his day would begin at 6.30a.m. by riding over the whole line (including the extension) to check that the track was in good order. He also took his turn on the late trams on Saturdays and always worked one weekend in two without extra pay.

Albert Edward "Jokey" Rhodes was employed on the construction of the tramway in 1895 and when the line opened he became a driver. His father was also employed by the company for a time.

In 1916 "Jokey" Rhodes joined the Royal Engineers and served in France. When the war finished he returned to the tramway, but finally left in the 1920's when he failed to receive a promised pay rise.

Albert "Jokey" Rhodes. 　　　　　Miss B. Rhodes Collection

Another employee who worked on the tramway for many years was Percy Sheppard who joined shortly before the First World War after his brother had left the company. Percy Sheppard was usually the conductor but did a little of everything including cleaning the carriages and polishing the brass work on the engines as well as relief driver. After the outbreak of the First World War he left to join the Army and when sent to France he met "Jokey" Rhodes.

When the war was over Percy Sheppard tried one or two other jobs before he rejoined the tramway in about 1920 and remained until its closure in 1939. He then joined the Southern Railway.

In the latter days of the line when the petrol engine was in use, the driver was mainly George Wratten who, with Percy Sheppard, made up the entire staff, although casual staff was normally taken on in the summer months. With the exception of a hat for the driver and the conductor, no other clothing was supplied. George Wratten became a familiar sight wearing a white yachting hat and light flannels while driving the petrol locomotive.

Conductor/guard Percy Sheppard (standing on the platform) and Albert "Jokey" Rhodes (driver) with 2-4-0T "Victoria" and both carriages at Camber Sands.

Many famous people used the tramway in connection with the Golf Club that, earlier in the century, held the Parliamentary Handicap which featured such well-known politicians of the day such as David Lloyd George, A.J. Balfour and the Hon. Alfred Lyttleton.

Well-known golfers like Henry Cotton (who was an assistant professional at Rye during the 1920's) and Cyril Tolley all made full use of the tramway in its heyday.

For the golfers who travelled from London, the tramway was the third leg in their journey to the golf course. Surprisingly, it was timed to link up with the London train from Brookland Station on the Dungeness/New Romney branch from Appledore. The middle leg of the journey between Brookland and Rye Tram Station being by coach.

An amusing anecdote from those times concerning the golfers and the tramway involved two young members of the club R.B. "Beau" Vincent, son of the Club Secretary and John Vidler, son of Trustee J.S. Vidler. These two younger members would often annoy the older members with their practical jokes and noisy behaviour in the carriage and on one Sunday evening, by way of a punishment, they were made to travel in the third class carriage. To get their own back the two youngsters decided to upset the plans for the London-bound travellers. As the tram waited at Golf Links Station the young Vincent and Vidler uncoupled the first/second class carriage which was at the rear. Surprisingly the driver left with only the third class carriage attached and arrived at Rye before realising that the first/second class carriage was missing. Fortunately (for the two young members anyway), a message had been sent to the Station-master at Brookland to hold the London train until the coach load of angry passengers arrived. (It's interesting to note that R.B. "Beau" Vincent went on to become a correspondent for "The Times" and that John Vidler became a Borstal and Prison Governor and also later became President of the Rye Golf Club).

2-4-0T "Camber" with the two open top passenger wagons and the Rother Ironworks carriage at Rye. 12th July 1922.

E.H. Robbins

One of the many photographs featuring a child standing on 2-4-0T "Camber"

Miss B. Rhodes Collection

Some young boys showing great interest in the petrol locomotive at Camber Sands Station. 11th April 1931.

H.C. Casserley

2-4-0T "Camber" with both carriages at Camber Sands.   Lens of Sutton

Golf Links Station on the 12th July 1931 looking towards Rye.   H.C. Casserley

The Final Years

In the late 1920's and the 1930's when many golfers owned their own cars and when a bus service started from Rye to Camber, the tramway began to feel competition for the first time like so many other similar light railways and country branch lines and entered a period of decline.

The company was now finding it increasingly difficult to balance the books although none of this was made obvious to the passengers who by now were mainly the Camber Sands day trippers.

In view of Camber becoming a growing seaside resort in the mid 1930's, the Southern Railway investigated the possibility of integrating the tramway into their system but, as the line's gauge was 3 ft and a connection with the main line at Rye across the River Rother would have been a major undertaking, the idea was dropped.

Just before the war started in 1939, a deviation to the tramway at Camber Sands had just been completed with the help of some unemployed men, but before it was brought into use war was declared and the line was closed, never again to be opened to the public.

At about this time W.E. Colebrooke & Co. Ltd., were digging out shingle on the Northpoint Beach. They had their own small 2 ft gauge railway which ran on a type of "jubilee" track. At one point this little railway went underneath the Rye & Camber Tramway track after a small bridge was built.

The bridge carrying the tracks of the Rye & Camber Tramway over the W.E. Colebrooke & Co. Ltd. Shingle Works Railway on the 19th April 1946.   S.C. Nash

Admiralty Use

During the Second World War, the Admiralty undertook a programme of civil engineering work based at Rye Harbour and built a continuous jetty about 1000ft long on the Camber side of the Rother near Golf Links Station from the Harbour Master's area towards Rye.

The tramway was requisitioned and brought back into service so that men and materials (mainly timber) for the work could be transported direct to the site from the Rye terminus. (The section of tramway from the Golf Links to Camber Sands was never used by the Admiralty).

Road access to the jetty was improved by concreting 2 strips from the main Camber-Rye road by the 11th green of the Golf Club and then by concreting on either side of the tramway track from Squatter's Right to the Golf Links Station where the passing loop was reinstated and a short siding to the jetty was added.

The contractors who carried out the work for the Admiralty were Mears Bros. Ltd., whose civil engineer was Mr. Jack Evans. The Admiralty engineer was Mr. Blofield.

When the work was completed, the jetty was fully operational with water supplied by a pipe-line which was laid on the bed of the river from a supply on the Rye Harbour side.

A large oil tank was also erected on the Rye Harbour side and oil was passed across the river by pipe.

When the war was over the line was returned to its owners but as the track and rolling stock was now in such a neglected state it was decided to wind up the company. This action went almost unobserved in Rye and by September 1947 the land that was leased from the Rye Council was surrendered and the Rye Tram Station was soon dismantled and the track taken up. "Camber" and the petrol locomotive were sold for scrap.

Looking back to Golf Links Station from the short siding which was laid to the Rother Pier. 19th April 1946.   S.C. Nash

Golf Links Station on the 19th April 1946 showing the concrete strips that the Admiralty laid each side of the track towards Rye and the concrete area in front of the platform, which includes the short branch to the Rother Pier on the left.   S.C. Nash

The dilapidated scene at Rye on the 19th April 1946 showing the Bagnall carriage, the original engine shed and the overgrown track all looking very neglected.   S.C. Nash

The remains of Camber Sands Station on the 19th April 1946.   S.C. Nash

The petrol locomotive outside the shed at Rye on the 19th April 1946. "Camber" can just
be seen inside the shed.   S.C. Nash

The Present Scene

Anyone looking for remains of the line today will be disappointed when they stand on the spot which was once the Rye Tram Station as there is no visible sign left to show that this was once the place where people set out on their journey across the marsh to either the Golf Club, Rye Harbour or Camber Sands. A pumping station now stands on the area once occupied by the original engine shed at the end of the line.

With the aid of a map you can just about pick up the rough outline of the route as you amble across the green fields where sheep roam without a care in the world.

On reaching Broadwater Stream it's nice to find that the two iron girders that once carried the tramway tracks are still in position and have found a different use by carrying a pipeline.

A short distance further on at the Northpoint Beach the shingle works which was once worked by W.E. Colebrooke & Co., and then G.T. Jennings & Co. Ltd., is now part of the Amey Roadstone Corporation and is partly flooded leaving no visible sign of the former tramway route.

At Gorse Cottage the route is picked up once more and by the site of Squatter's Right (which was demolished in 1983) you can find one or two wooden sleepers still in position. At this point the concrete strips which were laid during the last war are still intact and the original tramway rails are still there. Concrete has been added between the rails in some places as well.

The Golf Links Station building still survives and has been used in recent years as a store and, although the front of the building has been filled in with glass panels and the rear of the building slightly altered, there's no doubt that this building still has that certain look of a Col. Stephens Station.

The site of Rye Station looking towards the end of the line. 13th November 1984.   Author

The remains of Broadwater Bridge which now carries a pipeline instead of the tramway. 2nd October 1984.   Author

A modern day view of the remains of Golf Links Station with the front section of the building filled in. 2nd October 1984.   Author

From Golf Links Station it's quite easy to follow the alignment along the slight embankment until the site of Camber Sands Station is reached. Here you have to look very hard to find any remains, but a very close inspection reveals the wooden upright supports just sticking out of the sandy ground amongst some ferns.

Standing on the spot of the former Camber Sands Station today it's difficult to imagine what it must have been like on the 13th July 1908 when the extension was opened and also all those happy occasions when children would arrive with parents and friends for a day at the sea and on the sands.

The Bagnall carriage was saved from scrapping and was put to use as a summer house and then a chicken hut at East Guldeford near Rye.

During the mid 1960's the Brockham Museum Association near Dorking in Surrey were offered the chance to add this carriage to their collection even though the body frame, roof and wrought-iron frame were the only parts of the carriage still intact.

After very careful removal to Brockham, very little was done as it was obviously going to be a long term restoration job. Work was done on the frame from time to time and in 1982 it was removed to Chalk Pits Museum in Sussex after the amalgamation between the Brockham Museum and the Chalk Pits Museum.

This view is taken from the remains of Squatter's Right looking towards Golf Links Station. The track is still in position set in the concrete which was laid by the Admiralty during the last war. The concrete in between the rails was set at a later date. 13th November 1984.

Author

Conclusion

When the line was first opened there's no doubt that, apart from providing a novel form of transport, the tramway also provided the Golf Club, Rye Harbour and Camber Sands with a direct link with Rye.

This was to last until the 1920's and 1930's when competition was felt from road transport even though the road route was not so direct and with this competition in mind it is not surprising that the line was not reopened after the last war.

The pity of it is, that if it had survived, the "tram" would have been one of today's major attractions to Rye and certainly railway enthusiasts would travel from far and wide to see it.

To sit in the cosy atmosphere of one of the carriages on a cold or windy day or to experience the excitement of the open trucks rattling their way to Camber on a hot sunny day was no doubt a joy in itself, but unfortunately a joy that will never be experienced at Camber again.

2-4-0T "Victoria" with the two open top wagons and both carriages at Camber Sands.

Miss B. Rhodes Collection

2-4-0T "Camber" and both carriages at Rye.

Lens of Sutton

31

Acknowledgments

I would like to thank John Scott-Morgan for all the help and encouragement he gave me and for readily making his photographic collection available. Also many thanks to Jack Evans for all his help concerning the use of the tramway by the Admiralty during the last war and for walking the route with me. Thanks also to Philip Shaw for allowing me to make use of the "Tenterden Terrier" of which he is the editor.

I would also like to thank the following people and organisations for their kind help in compiling information and supplying photographs for this publication:

Mr. S.C. Nash, Mr. M. Lawson Finch, Lens of Sutton, Mr. K. Taylorson, Miss B. Rhodes, Mr. G.R. Croughton, Mr. H.C. Casserley, Mr. T. Middlemass, Mr. E.H. Robbins, Mr. D.A. Boreham, Mr. R.N. Innes, The L.C.G.B. for the Ken Nunn Collection, The Sussex Express and the East Sussex County Record Office.

My thanks to Mr. E.H. Peat for reading my text and also to Mr. J. Christian of Binfield Printers Ltd.

Bibliography

FORGOTTEN RAILWAYS: SOUTH-EAST ENGLAND by H.P. White.
THE RAILWAYS OF SOUTHERN ENGLAND: INDEPENDENT AND LIGHT RAILWAYS by Edwin Course.
RYE GOLF CLUB – THE FIRST 90 YEARS by Denis Vidler.
THE COLONEL STEPHENS RAILWAYS by John Scott-Morgan.
THE TENTERDEN TERRIER (Various issues).
THE RAILWAY MAGAZINE (Vol. 31. 1912 & Vol. 79. 1936).
TRAINS ILLUSTRATED (February 1972. Article by Alan A. Jackson).
SUSSEX COUNTY MAGAZINE (April 1932).
RYE'S OWN (September 1969).
BROCKHAM NEWS (Vol 2. No. 1).
NARROW GAUGE NEWS (October 1965).
W.L.I.A.S. JOURNAL (Christmas 1977).

All that remains of Camber Sands Station on the 13th November 1984. The ferns in the centre of the photograph mark the spot where the wooden platform once stood.   Author